How Paganism
and
Easy Believism

have

Infiltrated

The Christian Church

Robert M. Gullberg

Table of Contents

Media laden front stage of the modern church

Introduction to paganism- when Jesus walked the lands of Israel 2000 years ago, his primary opponents came from the leading religious leaders of his day, the Sadducees, and the Pharisees. Should it surprise us that history is repeating itself, and that the modern-day Christian church struggles in the errors of the religious educated? We have added traditions onto God's will for his church from the first century, and the church of New Testament Acts. As an active church goer for over 50 years, I keep wondering if I am the only one who notices the adulteration of the church today with secularism. Many church traditions are pagan in origin. Paganism is secularism, -meaning without God. Note that just because we use some traditions based on paganism does not make us pagans, but it can creep in and compromise us. Is it a wonder why some Christian churches have been somewhat ineffectual at times doing what God the Father wants us to do? "In the process of replacing the old religions, Christianity became a religion."- *Alexander Schmemann*

This book is a warning for all of us who attend our local churches week after week. Let's open our eyes wide to the possibility of compromise. So just what are some of the traditional clutter that we hold onto in the present-day church? To be discussed here include: **1) the church**

building 2) the Sunday morning service- how we do it 3) the sermon 4) the pastor, priest, or minister; "clergy" 5) the music, and 6) how we approach the issue of tithing.

Chapter 1 The church building- our culture is into special houses of worship, no question

about it. There seems to be a "love affair" with brick and mortar. However, there does not seem to be any biblical support for the church edifice. For example, I have seen enormous, beautiful Catholic cathedrals built in the 1950s in the jungles of the Congo, Africa left over from the Belgium colonials. Christians were never meant to meet in large buildings (see **1 Corinthians 3:16, 1 Timothy 3:15**), but in the early 300's A.D., Constantine, the emperor of Rome, erected the first church buildings throughout the Roman Empire. These buildings were patterned after the model of the basilica, designed after Greek pagan temples. They were good for seating passive crowds to watch performances. Christians have embraced the concept of the physical temple, made by human hands, where God dwells in a special way. Many churches are still built with steeples, which contradicts the message of the New Testament.

Christians do not have to "reach into the heavens" to find God. He is here! The church building no doubt requires a huge amount of mortgage money. Real estate owned by churches in the US alone numbers around $230 billion. It is estimated that building debt, service, and maintenance consumes about 18% of the $50-60 billion tithed to churches today. Think of what could be done with all that money for God's kingdom? Brick and mortar have hand-cuffed us. It tempts pastors to preach only "tickle-the-ears," candy-coated sermons to make people "feel good." I know of an evangelical church in a typical midwestern town in Wisconsin just finished paying off an $ 8 million dollar mortgage over the last 20 years. What could have been done in the community with that 8 million dollars.

The pulpit elevates the clergy to a position high above God's people. It puts the minister at center stage. I grew up in several mainline

denomination churches. The Evangelical

Swedish Covenant church, the Evangelical Free

Church, and two non-denominational Bible

churches. In each of these churches, the

ministers (head pastors and of music) sat on

elevated "thrones" in the front of the church

during the service. Grant it, the leaders

deserved respect, but this "king of the

congregation" approach can serve to cause

unscriptural hierarchy. The pulpit platform

or the worship area acts like a stage, and the

congregation occupies "the theatre." Pews and

balconies inhibit face-to-face fellowship. In a way, they have made corporate worship a "spectator sport."

Chapter 2 The Sunday morning service - most Sunday morning Protestant services at church are virtually identical. Variations are minor, even at "cutting edge" denominational churches. There seems to be a prescribed

"liturgy," even though it is not called that. This includes: *The Greeting (often with important announcements), Prayer or Bible reading, Worship songs, The Offering, The Sermon, and The*

Benediction. This tradition has been present for over 500 years. The roots of the Protestant order of service comes from the Catholic Mass. The Mass did not originate in the New Testament. The center of the Mass is the Eucharist. When Luther came along, he made preaching, rather than Communion the center of the church service. He started congregational singing. John Calvin led most of the service himself from the pulpit. Today, the pastor is the MC (Master of Ceremonies) or CEO of the Sunday morning service--just like the priest is the MC of the Catholic Mass. This is in stark contrast to the church meeting of the New Testament church. The contemporary church often uses the idea of "pragmatism" to attract people to church. Pragmatism depends on practical techniques ahead of God to produce the desired effects. This approach "opens the door" to human

 manipulation. In days past, D.L. Moody (1837-1899) added not only the "sinners' prayer" but also the "solo" hymn after the sermon which encouraged people to "come forward" to receive Jesus Christ. Today, seeker-sensitive churches have recognized the sterility of the present-day church service and thus have incorporated an array of media and theatre to "market" the service to the unchurched. Is this OK? Some would say "yes," some "no." The debate is ongoing.

Chapter 3 The sermon- remove the sermon from a weekly worship service and attendance is

sure to drop. The sermon is the "bedrock" of

the service (see John MacArthur giving his
sermon at Grace Community Church in
California). An entire service might be judged
by the "quality" of the sermon. The sermon is
delivered generally by the same person; the
pastor or ordained guest speaker. It is delivered
to a passive audience; basically, it is a
monologue. And it is presented in a "cultivated"
form of speech, and it usually has three points!
It is usually delivered with eloquence and
"polished rhetoric." As early as the 3rd century,
Christians called their sermons homilies, the

same term Greek orators used for their discourses. This can be contrasted to the kind of preaching mentioned in the Bible. Mutual exhortation and mutual teaching are key to spiritual transformation, and this cannot occur with our present system of church service. As believers, we must function if we are to mature in our faith (see **Mark 4:24-25, Hebrews 10:24-25**). We do not grow by passive listening to sermons week after week. The congregation becomes dependent on the clergy to "feed them." The sermon has little power to equip God's people. The feeding of the people that is happening in church today by sermons is likely not changing them.

Chapter 4 The clergy - your church may call the clergy a minister, pastor, reverend, or priest. There are more than 500,000 paid "leaders"

serving Christian churches in the US. Many
worship pastors make almost as much salary as
head pastors. Most clergy have Master's
degrees or Doctoral degrees and are highly
educated. In a way, the clergy and the pastoral
team in the church have put a dividing line
between them and the congregation. How? One
of the main thrusts of **Hebrews** is to end
the old priesthood. **1 Corinthians 12-14**
encourages members of the body the right and
privilege to minister. It has voided **1 Peter 2**
where everybody is a "functioning priest."
Viola says in the book *Pagan Christianity?* that it
has "rendered us a mute spectator who is

proficient at taking sermon notes and passing an offering plate." The present-day pastor was born out of the single-bishop spawned by Ignatius in about 100 AD. The bishop evolved into the local presbyter, and then in the Middle Ages, the presbyter grew into the Catholic priest. During the Reformation, he was changed into the preacher, minister, and finally the pastor.

This "CEO-type" position is grueling and has a high "burn-out" rate. The question is: did Jesus Christ ever intend any one person to "wear all the hats" of the present-day pastor? Should there be a single leader of the local church? Probably not. It is too stressful. Sunday morning special "dress-up" garb worn by clergy in many churches serve to separate them from their congregations, and it is rooted in secularism. In

Luke 20:46, Jesus says, "Beware of those who like to walk around in long robes." When those in the congregation wear flashy, attractive clothes at church, it is nothing more than "image management." Is it a reverence to God or just tradition? It hides the fact that the church is made up of real people with messy problems. You could never imagine Jesus or his disciples "dressing up" to separate them from God's people, could you?

Chapter 5 Music in the church - early church worship in the first century was in the hands of all of God's people. Singing and leading songs was corporate, not a professional event led by trained specialists. The jazziness of church bands and choirs has led to the "spectator mentality" of church. Is that what God intended with the local church? The origin of the "worship team" goes back to Chuck Smith's

Calvary Chapel in 1965. This ministry

originally was for surfers and hippies in

California. As the Jesus movement flourished,

Smith founded the Maranatha Music Company

in the early 1970's. The worship band replaced

the organ at that time. Although patterned after

the modern culture rock band, worship teams

are now as important to churches as the

preacher. The root of church choirs are found in

ancient Greek, pagan temples. The cultural

mind-set of the Greeks was built around this

audience-performance mentality. The formal

robes donned by many choir members in thousands of churches across the country gives people a false sense of pride and performance. Do we want corporate worship or entertainment?

Chapter 6 Tithing- the apostle Paul says in **2 Corinthians 2:17**, "Unlike so many, we do not peddle the word of God for profit." The problem

with "a tithe" today is that it can bring on resentment if most of the funds are often used to pay off mortgages for the brick and mortar of the church and not really for the work the church. Once the mortgage is paid off, it's time to spend more money on brick and mortar, or a new school, all well and good. The practice of tithing is in the Bible, but mostly in the Old Testament. There, a taxation system was needed to support the poor and priesthood who ministered for the Lord. But tithing is mentioned only four times in the New Testament, and it does not apply to present-day Christians. With the coming of Christ, the "old has been set aside" and rendered obsolete by the new. We are all priests now (**Hebrews 7:12-18, 8:13**). We are set free from the bondage of tithing. Like the first century Christians, we can give freely, out of a cheerful heart, without guilt, manipulation, or obligation, generously helping those in need (see **2 Corinthians 8:1-4, 9:6-7**).

Chapter 1 through 6 Study questions:

Describe how paganism has affected our Christian church today regarding:

The church building-

The Sunday morning service-

The sermon-

The clergy-

Music in the church-

Tithing-

Chapter 7 Easy believism- "Easy believism" or
"easier-to-believe-ism" is prevalent in today's
Christian church movement. It endeavors to
make Christianity and the Gospel "palatable" to
the American population (by the pragmatic, new
or "neo-evangelism"). The pastors of many
thousands of Christian churches are typically
dedicated people of faith and integrity.
However, beware- the "new evangelism"
philosophy which some espouse may lead to
shallow conversions to Christianity. Many
"easier-to-believers" think they are Christians,
but they were possibly never "saved" in the first
place. They "become" Christians and then they
place the "pursuit of holiness" on the back
burner. Could it be that many of these folks are

attending churches but may not be truly "born again?" Easier-to-believism has been perpetrated for several decades on print media, radio, and television by many famous Christian leaders. The danger: this approach may not promulgate the entire Gospel picture, and can yield a false, or "apostate," teaching. It is a compromised belief system that was born out of pressure from American culture. It focuses on the love of God for mankind manifested by his grace, and for some, "positive thinking" psychology, or "what sells." It does not teach about the truth of judgment, reality of hell, nor the "persistence of the saints."

Pick a trend---mega churches, satellite campuses, group ministries (to singles groups, women, men- i.e. Promise Keepers, young married), contemporary worship music, downloadable sermons, Alpha groups. All of these "programs" are attempts to rely on pragmatic "market" strategies to attract certain segments of the population to Christianity. Several aspects of "easier-to- believism" will be discussed here including: 1) "easier-to-believism" salvation 2) the seeker-sensitive church model (Willow Creek Church or Rick Warrens' Saddleback Church) 3) "feel-good self-esteem" taught by the likes of Norman Vincent Peele, Robert Schuller, and Joel Osteen 4) the ecumenical (worldwide religious unity) movement, show-cased for example, by the late Billy Graham in his "crusades" or Franklin Graham "festivals."

Chapter 8 Salvation- Colossians 1:21-23a says it best. "Once you were alienated from God and were enemies in your minds because of your evil behavior. But now he has reconciled you by Christ's physical body through death to present you holy in his sight, without blemish and free from accusation--if you continue in your faith, established and firm, not moved from the hope held out in the gospel." In other words, if we are truly born again, we will continue in the faith. There is no salvation without repentance. If we do not continue in the faith, maybe we were never saved in the first place. If a person is living in constant sin, he is lost. "Carnal Christians" was a name invented given to believers who constantly backslide into their sinful lifestyles. A true Christian may fall into sin, but he or she will not live in sin; there is a difference. **Titus 2:13** says, "For the grace of God teaches us to say "no" to ungodliness and worldly passions, and to live self-controlled, upright and godly lives in this present age."

Those who possess eternal life by the grace of God, obey him. "And why call me Lord, Lord, and do not do the things that I say?"- **Luke 6:46.** **John 15:14** says, "You are my friends if you do what I command." In **Luke 13:3**, Jesus said, "I tell you, unless you repent, you too will perish."

Note that we do not keep ourselves saved by obeying him, but obedience is simply proof that we are his sheep. In discussing those who have "superficially" turned to Christ and then fallen away, Peter says in **2 Peter 2:19-22**, "they themselves are slaves of depravity--for a man is a slave to whatever has mastered over him. If they have escaped the corruption of the world by knowing our Lord and Savior Jesus Christ and are again entangled in it and over-come, they are worse off at the end than they were at the beginning. It would have been better for them not to have known the way of righteousness than to have known it and then to turn their backs on the sacred command that was passed on to them. Of them the proverbs are true: "A dog returns to its vomit," and "A sow that is washed goes back to her wallowing in the mud." Satan is great at getting folks to make false professions that will not hold up under pressure. Authentic Christians hang in there and persist in their faith. **Romans 6:16-18** says, "Being then made free from sin, you became the servants of righteousness."

Chapter 9 Seeker sensitive church model- Willow Creek Community Church (WCCC) in a northwestern suburban Chicago and Saddleback Church in California are examples of mega (super-large) churches which seek the lost by being "sensitive" to cultural relevance. When

Bill Hybels, who had been the senior pastor of
WCCC in South Barrington Illinois, started the

church back in the 1970s, he asked people in the
community who were un-churched what
"turned them off" about attending church. The
survey showed that people: 1) didn't like being
bugged for money 2) found church routine and
predictable 3) didn't think that church was
relevant to their lives and 4) always left church
feeling guilty. Hybels answer was to program
the weekend "seeker service" to non-believers
and the mid-week "New Community" service to
believers.

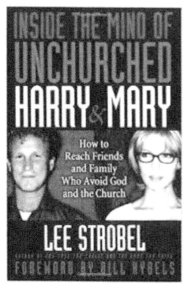

Willow Creek's goal was to introduce the "un-churched Harry's and Mary's" to a creative, introductory level, positive, Bible-centered church experience. The idea was to give the un-churched people what they wanted. These included: 1) anonymity 2) introductory level truth 3) time to "make a decision" and 4) excellent programming including creativity, humor, contemporary cutting edge worship music, drama, relevancy, etc. (source from Hybels' 1990 message: "Who we are at Willow Creek"). WCCC has had up to six weekend services, two geared for younger generations. The original church meets in a

352,000-square-foot building that seats 4,500, located on a 155-acre campus (a new building was added for $80 million). An article describes a service at Willow creek as "a slick, show-biz service where drama and soft rock music are served up on a stage washed in pink and blue spotlights. A soft-sell sermon is delivered from a lucite lectern...the people attending will not be bored as a combination of drama, humor, and pop music is presented with no archaic hymns."

Let us not lose sight of the fact that Willow Creek Community Church has done a ton of good for the community. They have raised millions of dollars for the poor. They are active in missions. They have had thousands of small groups. They have a support program for literally every problem one can think of. Their growth has been phenomenal. If success was measured in numbers, they seemed to have done something right.

So, are there warnings regarding the "seeker-sensitive" model? Yes. At least four. 1) Being "light" on the total doctrine of Christianity and not looking more seriously at the costs of following Jesus and the costs of *not* following him (i.e. being separated from God eternally in hell). 2) Not being fully devoted followers of Jesus Christ. Attenders yes. Fully committed, maybe not. The tendency can be to associate oneself more with the seeker-sensitive mega church, than with Jesus Christ. 3) It "buys into" the idea of Christian consumerism (what can the church do for me?). 4) It can build church attendees that are a "mile wide and an inch thick" in terms of "their walk," and tempts compromise to worldly principles.

One-half of the attendees at WCCC are from a Catholic background. This tells us a few things. WCCC has something the Catholic Church does not have. Is it the casual "come as you are" attitude or the lack of liturgy that is perhaps a breath of fresh air for this group? The Catholic Church has been heavy on following tradition of the Mass and on "good works" salvation. Because of this, folks of the Catholic tradition (but not just Catholics really) often deal with a lot of guilt if they do not keep "up to par" with expectations. Therefore, WCCC is a safe harbor for them. Little tradition. No liturgy. And certainly, no guilt with the "soft sell" approach to Christianity.

Saddleback Church in Lake Forest, California, like Willow Creek Community Church is one of the most influential churches in the world. Rick

Warren says, "This is a world class church making a world class impact." He has taught over 300,000 pastors through his church growth seminars, and far more through his books. His influence stretches across all Christian denominations. "The Purpose Driven Life" (sequel to *The Purpose Drive Church*) has sold more than 4.5 million copies. What is a worship service like at Saddleback Church? Similar to Willow Creek, Warren says "I believe that one of the major church issues of the future will be how we're going to reach the next generation with our music…baby boomers want to feel the music, not just hear it…" Is that what Jesus wants us to do? If it is music that brings us to faith, why didn't Jesus get 12 top-notch musicians to be his apostles and just sing to the masses? If a sinner does not care about the Word of God, there isn't a song in the world that can save him. It has been noted that a minority of attendees bring a Bible to church. Warren's messages are motivational challenges for people to dedicate themselves to God. The chief error is in the things that are not stated, which is the hallmark of neo-evangelism. This evangelism neglects the full truth of the Gospel as it tries to present the Bible in a more positive light. It can "shallow" the absolute truths of Scripture. Avoiding doctrinal controversy is key (being politically correct) to Saddleback's success. Warren says, "I'm not going to get into a debate over the non-essentials. I will not try to change other denominations. Why be divisive?"

He tickles the ears of his congregation with a positive-only, non-offensive message. The same generation that hates the uncompromising, plainly spoken fundamentalist-style preaching clearly loves the Rick Warrens and the Billy Grahams and the Joel Osteen's of the Christian world.

Chapter 10 Feel good philosophy- Norman Vincent Peale wrote "The Power of Positive Thinking" in 1952, and more than 20 million copies have been sold since then. It has been the model for self-help, self-esteem, and self-recovery books ever since. He and his wife started "Guideposts" in 1945, and its circulation tops millions, the largest of any religious magazine (there is mention about God in

Guideposts, but not Jesus Christ). He pastored New York City's Marble Collegiate Church for 52 years and the church grew from 600 members

to 5000 members when he retired in 1984. For 54 years, his radio program "The Art of Living" was broadcast on NBC. He is the person responsible for bringing psychology into the Christian church. He advocated liberal teachings such as visualization, positive imaging, pantheism, human potential, and of course positive thinking. On a 1984 Phil Donahue Show, Peale, a 33rd degree Mason, said, "It's not necessary to be born again (to obtain salvation). You have your way to God, I have mine. I found eternal peace in a Shinto shrine. I have been to Shinto shrines and God is everywhere...Christ is (only) one of the

ways! Just so we think good thoughts and just so we do good, we believe we'll get to heaven." (*Sword of the Lord*, 12/14/1984)

Peale rejected the virgin birth of Jesus, the doctrine of sin, and that Christ was eternal God. God is never presented as a Judge in Peale's writings. Peale's faith was not faith in God, but "faith in faith," which means faith in your own capacities as a means in attaining the well-adjusted life (*Christian News*; 1/3/1994) The Christ that Peale preached was very much like Alcoholics Anonymous founder Bill Wilson's ambiguous "Higher Power" (*Christianity Today*; 6/21/1993).

Robert Schuller has been one of Norman Vincent

Peale's most "successful" protégés. On

Schuller's 1000th anniversary television show,

"The Hour of Power," aired on 4/2/1989,

Schuller's son said that Peale was "responsible

for dad's possibility thinking." His television

ministry at one time had taken in $50

million/year and is beamed to 20 million people

in 180 countries. Nobody is a better salesman

than Schuller on TV selling Christian trinkets or

memorials to fund his ministry. Yet, Schuller

teaches that there is no need for one to recognize

his own personal sin (sin is merely the lack of

self-esteem), no need for repentance, and no need for the crucifixion of self. To him, the self is to be exalted. Schuller says, "Jesus knew his worth; his success fed his self-esteem. He suffered the cross to sanctify his self-esteem and he bore the cross to sanctify your self-esteem. The cross will sanctify the ego trip" (from his book, "Self-Esteem: The New Reformation"). Schuller is a universalist (cloaked in Christendom) who believes that all people are the children of God. Schuller says, "We try to focus on not offending those with different view-points."

Today, Joel Osteen is pastor of the nondenominational Lakewood Church in Houston, Texas. This congregation has more than 30,000 members, and its 2004 revenue was $55 million. Osteen's book of human-potential, self-esteem, feel- good, self-help-guide titled,

"Your Best Life Now: Seven Steps to Living at

Your Full Potential" ranked number one on the

New York Times best-seller list. Osteen's

message is described as, "a simple self-help

message that congregants say is both uplifting

and accessible...he proudly wears the

title of 'the smiling preacher.' His theology has

been called 'cotton candy;' it tastes good, but

there is little substance. On a Larry King Live

interview on June 20th, 2005, Osteen refused to

confess that Jesus Christ was the only way of

salvation. After the interview, he got so much

negative feedback from well-meaning Christians in his congregation that he wrote a letter apologizing for his "lack of clarity" when it came to his true faith in Christ alone. Osteen's "politically correct" preaching, like Peale's and Schuller's, attracts a lot of people, but does it lack the complete Gospel Message?

Chapter 11 The ecumenical movement- perhaps unknowingly, Billy Graham and

his crusades have perpetrated the ecumenical movement (the bringing together of different religions) in today's world. Graham, born in 1918, was an ordained Southern Baptist minister. He headed a $100 million a year evangelistic empire called the Billy Graham Evangelistic Association (BGEA). Graham's magazine, *Decision*, reached 1.7 million people and many of his books have been best-sellers (such as *Angels*, in 1975). Graham preached to over 200 million people and once claimed that precisely 2,874,082 of them have stepped forward to "accept Jesus Christ as personal Savior" (11/15/1993 Time magazine). Who's counting? Franklin Graham told the *Indianapolis Star* on 6/3/1999 that his father's longstanding ecumenical alliance with the Catholic Church and all other denominations, "was one of the smartest things his father ever did." Billy has even been quoted as saying, "Anyone who makes a decision at our meetings is seen later, followed up and referred to a local clergyman, Protestant, Catholic, or Jewish." Graham's call to "receive Christ," or "make the step of faith," or "come to Christ tonight," is general enough to "allow Catholic leaders to insert their sacramental gospel into it." In the fall of 1992, he was asked for his position on homosexuality (Oregon was having an upcoming statewide referendum that would declare homosexuality abnormal and would thereby prohibit government support of it). Rather than giving a clear Biblical answer, Graham played the politician. "I find it is emotional. I stay out of politics. God loves all people whatever their ethnic or political background or their social orientation... Christians on both sides of the issue must love each other...I never speak against other groups" (9/22/1992 *The Statesman Journal*). On the 12/22/1994 Larry King Live Show, Graham said that he believed that homosexuals are born with a tendency toward homosexuality. Graham seemed to avoid controversy at any cost at times. Perhaps most important was Graham's attitude regarding religions with false teaching. In 1948, he said: "The three gravest menaces faced by Orthodox Christianity are Communism, Roman Catholicism, and Islam." By 1973, however, Graham said that communist Mao Tse-Tung's "eight precepts are basically the same as the Ten Commandments," he praised the Roman Catholic Mass as beautiful, and said Mohammed Ali's beliefs in Islam "are something we all could believe." In 1985, Graham affirmed his belief that those who do not believe in Jesus Christ as their Savior might be saved. When asked, "What about people of other faiths who live good lives but don't profess a belief in Christ?" Graham replied, "I'm going to leave that to the Lord. He'll decide that" (*Los Angeles*

Herald Examiner, 7/22/1985). Is this a compromise
of the truth of the Bible? He repeated this theme
in a television interview with Robert Schuller on
5/31/1998. Graham said, "God is calling people
out of the world for his name, whether they
come from the Muslim world, or the Buddhist
world, or the Christian world, or the non-
believing world, they are members of the Body
of Christ because they have been called by God.
They may not even know the name of Jesus, but
they know in their hearts that they need
something that they don't have, and they turn to
the only light that they have, and I think that
they are saved, and that they're going to be with
us in heaven." In 1993, Graham attended a
prayer breakfast in which President Clinton
participated. Senator Kerry read John 3:1-21 and
skipped 3:16. Kerry said, "Christ was speaking
of spiritual renewal and that in the spirit of

Christ...Hindu, Buddhist, Muslim, Jew, Christian.... we're meeting and there is a renewal here." Billy Graham added, "I do not know a time when we had a more spiritual time than we've had today." Reverend Graham seemed to be interested in being spiritual than being correct doctrinally about the absolute truth of salvation through Christ alone.

Not to be discussed here are Billy Graham's support of: 1) "being made a Christian through infant baptism" (10/10/1961, *The Lutheran Standard*) 2) that hell is not a literal place but just "separation from God" (*Time magazine*, 11/15/1993) 3) believing in the virgin birth of Christ not being necessary for personal salvation (*United Church Observer*, 7/1/1966) 4) that sex may be present in Heaven if sex is necessary for one's happiness and fulfillment; in fact, anything that is necessary for one's happiness will be there (CNN; *Larry King Live,* 12/25/1998) 5) the Bible being inspired and authoritative but <u>not inerrant</u>. "I don't use the word "inerrant" because it's become a divisive word." (*Newsweek* magazine; 4/26/1982) and 6) the Williamsburg Charter Foundation (WCF no longer exists but the curriculum has been passed to "The First Liberty Institute") which promotes religious tolerance in education and a new, world religion (6/25/1988). For antidotes to "Easy Believism", read *The Explicit Gospel* by Matt Chandler or *The Gospel for Real Life* by Jerry Bridges.

Conclusion to this book

This short book is simply a warning for all of us Christians who live in the 21st century. Regarding the paganism creeping into the present-day church, our spirits must be pricked as to the disguises that Satan can wear as he tempts us in our churches to be too comfortable with our culture. The book is not about bashing the philosophies of Bill Hybels, Rick Warren, Norman Vincent Peale, Robert Schuller, Joel Osteen, and Billy Graham. These strong and charismatic leaders have all had unique and different ministries. In fact, each man has done a 'heap of good' in world in many ways. Each has left an indelible mark. But that is not the point of this book. Sometimes, we Christians can 'get drunk' with the celebrity status of our leaders. Sometimes we forget what we stand for. It's all about Jesus Christ and what He did for us to give us salvation. He is our celebrity!

Chapter 7 through 11 Study questions:

Define "easier-to-believism." Discuss its dangers.

Describe four important aspects of the "seeker-sensitive" church model.

1)

2)

3)

4)

Describe the "feel-good" self-esteem philosophy, and Normal Vincent Peele's and Robert Schuller's approach to Christianity.

Discuss the tenets of the ecumenical movement and Billy Graham.

Notes for application for your life:

About the author

Robert M. Gullberg is originally from Park Ridge, Illinois and has practiced Internal Medicine in Racine, Wisconsin for over three decades. His father was a dentist and practiced for over 40 years, many of those years as a volunteer at the Pacific Garden Mission in Chicago, Illinois. Both of his parents- Robert C. and Adrienne, as well as brother Jim, and sisters Lin and Lauri have been believers and influenced him in the Christian faith.

He has attended evangelical Christian churches in the Midwest for over 50 years. His journey with the Lord began as a 13-year-old at the Northwest Covenant Church in Mt. Prospect, Illinois. There, Pastor Engseth led him to the Lord. While attending Maine East High School, mentorship from Dave Veerman of Campus Life followed. Son City at South Park Church with Bill Hybels as Youth Pastor was part of his growing experience. When college began, Craig Domeck took him under his wing in Campus Crusade for Christ. Medical school followed, and some warm fellowship with regular Bible Studies was part of the weekly spiritual diet. While in Rockford, Illinois on a three-year medical stint, he attended the Evangelical Free

Church. Dr. Dave Norquist was a special friend, and quality time was spent with the Christian Medical Society group, as well as with Eric Anderson, his travel mate to India. Post-graduate training followed at Northwestern University, and Bible studies with cross-healthcare students kept him active in God's word. Small group studies with Peter Jaggard, M.D., Doug Smith, Steve Bundra M.D. and many others were regular. When Bob arrived in Racine, Wisconsin to start his medical practice, the late Dr. Jim Peterson and Dr. Don Cohill mentored him for years. Presently, Dr. Bob and his family have been active in an evangelical church in southeast Wisconsin for decades. He tributes Pastor Jerry Worsham, Pastor Rusty Hayes, and Reverend John Schindler having an impact on his life from the pulpit for a span of three decades.   Dr. Bob has led Bible studies for decades on all sorts of topics from Genesis to Revelation.

 He has had the opportunity to do short term medical work in several remote areas of the world doing medical missions including Honduras, Haiti, and central Africa. God is at work in every nook and cranny of this globe. He has been a practicing internist for years and has kept busy trying to take care of a full load of patients. There are occasions daily to see God work His miracles in his patients.

One of his goals in life is to get know the Bible like he knows his profession of medicine (however, the more he knows in these areas, the more he realizes that he has a lot to learn)! He hopes your goal is similar; to know the heartbeat of God through the Scriptures.

He has written *Principles for the Christian Life: Bible Study Edition*, *Wisdom from the Word*, *Encountering Grace: A 50-Chapter Bible study of Genesis*, *Know What the Future Holds: A Study on the Book of Revelation*, *Practical Insights for Living: 40 Bible Studies from Proverbs*, *Get a Jump on Life: Proverbs for Teens*, *and the nine-volume series called Proverbs for Kids*.

Printed in Great Britain
by Amazon